THE SOLDIER THROUGH THE AGES
THE CIVIL WAR
RIFLEMAN

Martin Windrow

Illustrated by
Jeffrey Burn

Franklin Watts
New York   London   Toronto   Sydney

© Franklin Watts Limited 1985

First published in Great Britain in 1985 by
Franklin Watts Ltd
12a Golden Square
London W1

First published in the USA by
Franklin Watts Inc.
387 Park Avenue South
New York
N.Y. 10016

First published in Australia by
Franklin Watts Australia
1 Campbell Street
Artarmon
NSW 2064

UK edition ISBN: 0 86313 298 7
US edition ISBN: 0-531-10081-2
Library of Congress Catalog Card
No: 85-50762

Designed by James Marks

Printed in Belgium

Contents

The North versus the South

From 1861 to 1865 the United States of America was torn apart by a cruel civil war between the Northern and Southern states. The North (the Federal or Union forces) fought for the national government of President Abraham Lincoln. The South fought for the independence of a split-off Confederacy of eleven rebel states under Jefferson Davis.

The reasons for the outbreak of war were many and complicated. The most talked-about issue was the South's use of black slave labor in cotton plantations; but the real causes lay much deeper. The basic argument was over the rights of the national government as against the rights of individual state governments.

In 1865 the North forced the remaining Southern soldiers to surrender. The North was much richer in men, money and industrial factories to build the tools of war. But the Southern soldiers were so brave and so well led that the war did not end before both sides had suffered terrible losses.

▷ A Northern soldier (left) with the stars and stripes flag and a Southern soldier (right) with the stars and bars. The richer Union army issued only a simple blue fatigue uniform. If the Confederate soldier wore a uniform at all, it was a makeshift gray or brown outfit which often included captured Union items.

Although there was some enforced service, most men on both sides were true volunteers, fighting for their beliefs. About 70 per cent were under 23 years old; nearly 10 per cent were only 16 *or younger*, and some were just 10 or 12 years old. Most were farmhands or laborers of British, German or Scandinavian descent. Sketchily trained and disciplined, but tragically brave, they filled half a million graves in just four years.

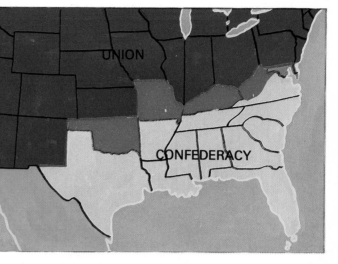

△ The Confederate states were North and South Carolina, Georgia, Alabama, Mississippi, Texas, Louisiana, Florida, Arkansas, Tennessee and Virginia. Some "slave" states (shown here in red) did not join the Confederacy and were disputed ground, with men on both sides.

About 3½ million men wore the uniform of one side or the other. Hundreds of thousands never actually saw a battle, yet of this total one in seven died and one in seven was wounded. This was at least as bad a casualty rate as that suffered by the British army in World War I.

One reason for the appalling losses was the inexperience of the men. The pre-war US army numbered only 16,000, but on the outbreak of war hundreds of thousands of raw volunteers enlisted in both armies. Most regiments had only a handful of experienced officers and sergeants to train the new recruits.

In many ways this was the first "modern" war. It saw the first major use of railways to transport men and supplies; signaling by electric telegraph; trading ports blockaded by armored ships; aerial reconnaissance from hydrogen balloons; even the first use of true machine guns.

The chain of command

A few of the volunteers who enlisted in 1861 had some part-time experience in their state militias. These local defense organizations were more like social clubs. They had fancy uniforms, bands and smart drill parades – but little realistic battle training. Most of the "civilians in uniform" who fought in the first campaigns were quite ignorant about warfare – and this included the thousands of hastily appointed officers. Many men marched into their first battle without ever having fired their guns, even in practice.

The few pre-war army officers, divided between North and South, were in great demand and were often promoted very quickly. The Confederate cavalry commander Jeb Stuart was a general at the age of twenty-nine. Sadly these dashing young leaders often found themselves fighting old friends. (Even President Lincoln had close relatives in the Confederate Army.)

The diagram on the opposite page shows how regiments were organized into brigades, divisions and corps. An army on

◁ A Union general. Officers' rank badges were worn on gold-braided straps across the shoulders, but otherwise senior ranks enjoyed great freedom of dress.

▷ From 1863 Union troops wore hat patches identifying their corps (by shape) and division (by color).
Red heart: 1st Div., XXIV Corps. White Maltese Cross: 2nd Div., V Corps. Blue diamond: 3rd Div., III Corps. Green six-point star: 4th Div., VIII Corps.

campaign consisted of several corps. But because all units were much weaker than their official strength, especially on the Union side, a corps which should have had about 30,000 men often numbered only about 12,000 or 15,000.

Units from the same or neighboring states were often brigaded together. As a result many men knew their fellow soldiers and officers from civilian life. This helped to build up trust between men and units fighting alongside one another.

The South was always better than the North at keeping units together for long periods. They also had a better system of replacing casualties. Recruits were regularly sent to top up weakened Rebel regiments. Units built up traditions which were good for the men's confidence, and the veterans could teach the newcomers their skills. But Union regiments were often allowed to dwindle away. They were then disbanded and replaced by completely fresh and inexperienced units. This was not only inefficient, but was bad for morale.

▷ This diagram of the Union VI Corps, 1865, shows how the individual regiment fitted into the army's command system:

The **regiment**, here the 2nd New Jersey Volunteer Infantry, was made up of ten **companies**. Each officially had 100 men; but death, disease and deserters often reduced regiments from 1,000 to nearer 300 or 400 men.

Officially, four regiments made a **brigade**. In fact, five or six regiments might be brigaded together to make up the numbers – and might still field only some 1,500 men, instead of the required 4,000.

Three brigades made a **division**. Three divisions and an artillery brigade made a **corps**, led by a major-general. The VI Corps (badge: a Greek cross in red, white or blue for the 1st, 2nd and 3rd Divisions) had 44 regiments instead of the official 36, but was probably still below half its official strength.

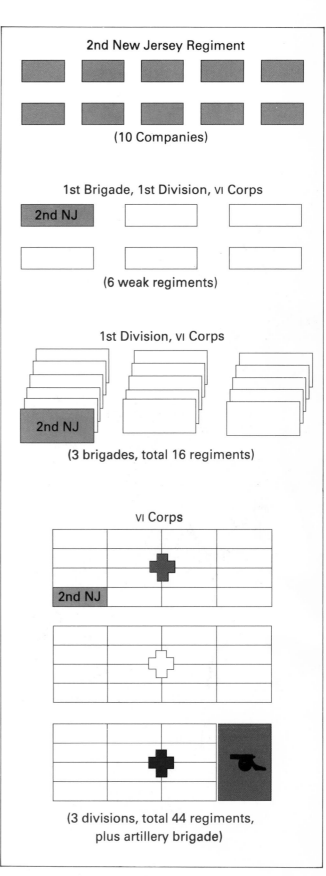

2nd New Jersey Regiment

(10 Companies)

1st Brigade, 1st Division, VI Corps

2nd NJ

(6 weak regiments)

1st Division, VI Corps

2nd NJ

(3 brigades, total 16 regiments)

VI Corps

2nd NJ

(3 divisions, total 44 regiments, plus artillery brigade)

Fancy dress and homespun

The Civil War armies are often referred to as "the Blue and the Gray." In fact, although most Union troops *did* wear blue, and there *was* an official Confederate uniform of gray, an astonishing variety of clothes was worn by soldiers on both sides.

The first campaigns were fought mostly by the militia regiments of the various states. Since they were a law unto themselves, many militia units ordered exotic uniforms copied from foreign styles that caught their fancy. In the 1850s the French army had a great reputation for dash and style. The colorful uniforms of France's African colonial units were thought very elegant, and the first battles of the Civil War saw many regiments dressed in the turbans, fezzes, bolero jackets and baggy trousers of far-off Algeria! (Some units kept these special uniforms right through the war, but many found them too expensive in the long run.)

Union factories turned out plain blue "sack" jackets, sky-blue trousers and many

▷ Union uniforms (left to right):
Berdan's Sharpshooters carried Sharps rifles and wore traditional rifleman's green.
The 146th New York Regiment was one of several units who wore French Zouave uniform throughout the war.
The pre-war regulation dress of the US Regular Infantry; drummers had fancy coat-braiding.

varieties of the jaunty fatigue cap. Badges were usually limited to stripes on the arms for corporals and sergeants. The South, on the other hand, was too poor to issue its entire army with identical dress. (Its whole industry was less than half the size of that of the Union state of New York.) The Confederate states did the best they could, no two dressing their men exactly alike. Many Confederate soldiers wore some kind of gray jacket, but most had only a drab brown uniform dyed with "butternut."

The typical Southern soldier wore a makeshift outfit of gray, brown, civilian or captured Union clothing and a big "slouch" hat. Southern soldiers hated carrying more than the absolute minimum of equipment. They would rather throw away anything they did not need, trusting to luck to find, say, a discarded coat once the weather actually turned cold, rather than carry one during the summer. They rolled their equipment in a blanket slung around their shoulders.

◁ Confederate uniforms (left to right): Regulation Confederate Infantry uniform was not much seen after 1862. Typical mixture of items worn by a Maryland Infantry corporal: the black cross was a Maryland badge. Zouave-style uniform of the Louisiana Tigers, an Irish regiment from New Orleans. They also had a red-trimmed brown jacket.

Weapons and equipment

The most important difference between the Civil War foot soldiers and their counterparts in the Napoleonic period was the improved and more accurate gun. The rifle-musket was still loaded through the muzzle. A paper cartridge holding the gunpowder and bullet was pushed down the barrel with an iron rod. But the bullet was now conical, not round; and the barrel was not smooth inside, but had a spiral groove, or rifling. These changes made the bullet spin as it flew, which kept it traveling in a straight line. The old smooth-bore was unable to hit even a big target at more than about 150 paces; the rifle-musket was deadly at up to 500 paces in the hands of a trained man.

It was also more reliable because of its percussion lock. The old musket had been fired by a device which struck a wedge of flint against a steel plate, dropping the sparks into a little open powder pan on the outside of the gun. As a result the gun did not always fire in wind or rain. The new percussion cap was a tiny copper-covered pellet of explosive which fitted on a thin tube on the side of the gun. A hammer dropped on the cap and set it off; sparks shot through the little tube, into the powder charge rammed down inside the barrel. Because the sparks were kept *inside* the gun, protected from the weather, this system was much more reliable.

Apart from his gun, ammunition and bayonet, the rifleman's equipment was very simple: food, water, cooking and eating utensils, blankets, a few clean clothes, and – if he was lucky – tent canvas and a waterproof groundsheet. A Northern soldier was issued a knapsack to carry it all in; but he often managed to "lose" it and copied his enemy's blanket-roll!

◁ **1** Spare clothes, blankets and a canvas tent-half rolled up in a gum blanket. The soldier could button his tent-half to a friend's to make a small, two-man shelter rigged over their guns and bits of cord. The rubber-coated gum blanket served as a rain cape and groundsheet.

2 Waterproofed with tar, the haversack had an inner cotton bag for carrying food – which often got mixed together in a greasy mess!

3 Tin water canteen with a cloth cover, marked by the owner.

4 Big mugs were useful both for cooking and eating.

△ **5** Springfield rifle-musket carried by Union soldiers. The rifleman tore the paper cartridge with his teeth, poured the powder into the muzzle, then rammed the bullet and paper down on top of it. Lastly he fitted the percussion cap on to the little tube at the breech and pulled the hammer back ready for firing.

6 Pouch containing 40 paper cartridges.

7 Belt, with percussion cap pouch and bayonet. Bayonets were used more often for digging than for fighting.

8 Union sergeants wore a sword and sash as marks of rank.

Camp life

The Civil War rifleman spent more time in camp than on campaign. While marching over the countryside in summer, a squad of eight or ten men shared a tent. In winter they camped in a rough cabin. These were often quite cozy, with home-made furniture and chimneys made from barrels. Muddy paths were paved with logs, and *some* effort was made to keep conditions reasonably clean and sanitary!

When the overworked supply service actually managed to deliver food, Northern rations were quite varied. They included pork or beef; flour or hard biscuit-bread; rice or sometimes potatoes; peas or beans; coffee or tea; sugar, salt, pepper, vinegar and molasses.

The Southern soldier was much worse off. Records of 1863 show he received only a little bacon, flour, peas, sugar and salt. Both sides "foraged" (in other words, stole from farmers' fields), but both were short of fresh vegetables, and this led to bad health. Out of sight of their officers, outpost sentries on each side used to swop Northern coffee for Southern tobacco.

If a rifleman had the money, he could buy small luxuries from the sutler. This was a

◁ A man caught stealing is kept tied up for hours, wearing a shameful placard and gagged with a bayonet. America's volunteer soldiers could not simply be frightened into obedience by such punishments as whipping. They had to be persuaded that rules were just and sensible.

THIEF

trader who set up shop from a wagon or cabin to sell things like cheese, candy, fruit, canned food, razors, pens, paper and sewing kit – but strictly no alcohol.

The soldiers in camp got bored, and discipline suffered. Independent-minded Americans did not take kindly to rigid rules: they drank, talked back and brawled! More seriously, many thousands deserted from both armies. After a campaign they felt they had done their work and saw no reason why they should not go home to help get the harvest in. A few unlucky ones were shot as an example, but it did little good.

▽ In winter camp Yanks line up by a cookhouse made in the chimney of a ruined house. Others prefer to cook their rations with a few friends. (If for any reason fires could not be lit, a popular snack was raw pork and sugar between two biscuits!) In the background is a sutler's cabin. Prices were supposed to be controlled; but being the only shop in town, the sutler often overcharged the men.

S. UNSTEAD
SUTLER
180ᵀᴴ N.Y. VOLS

NO TICK

Southern raiders

Horses played a major part in the Civil War, both as cavalry mounts and to move men and supplies. The North alone used 800,000 horses (even though they had many more railway tracks than the South and often moved men and supplies by train).

At first the South had more skilled cavalry than the North. Their use of this advantage often brought the Northern soldier face to face with his enemy while he was still far behind the battle lines.

Most Southerners took easily to cavalry fighting and they had several brilliant leaders, like Jeb Stuart, John Morgan and Nathan Forrest. These proud leaders were expert at raiding deep into Union territory. They scouted Union troop movements and drove off Union patrols, "blinding" Union generals to the maneuvers of Southern armies. They tore up the rail tracks upon which the North depended. They burned or carried off huge amounts of Union stores, ambushed convoys and wrecked vital bridges.

In October 1862 Stuart's famous Chambersburg Raid rode around the Union army, covering 80 miles (130 km) in 27 hours and capturing 1,200 Union horses. On such raids the troopers might spend as much as twenty-one hours a day in the saddle. Shortage of mounts was a problem for the South. Each trooper provided his horse, but although he was paid expenses, it was not replaced if it died. The longer the war dragged on the harder it became to keep up Confederate cavalry strength.

▽ Confederate cavalry loot a derailed Union supply train and cut telegraph wires to stop the crew from calling for help when they leave. They carry off food, guns and anything of use – even new boots and trousers! They were so skilled at raiding Union supplies, and so short of many necessities, that they actually used to plan on filling their needs in this way when they began a campaign. In wild country the North could not guard every track against them.

15

The cruel arithmetic of attack

2 Companies in reserve

300 yd

6 Companies (main force)

1,500 yd–650 yd : 10 min : 20 shells or spherical case

When the rifleman finally faced his enemy in pitched battle, he suffered an ordeal as terrible as anything his forefathers had experienced in earlier ages of warfare. New inventions made his weapons more accurate and destructive than those of the Napoleonic Wars – the last important campaigns between European-style armies before the 1860s, and the example which most generals copied. As tactics had hardly changed at all to keep pace with the improved weapons, battle was horribly dangerous for the soldier in the ranks.

△ Attackers advancing at a slow pace had to endure artillery fire for up to 15 minutes before reaching the enemy. The diagram shows how many shots of different kinds could be fired at them during this time. Exploding shells; spherical case (shrapnel), which burst in mid-air, throwing out musket balls; and solid roundshot cannon balls, were all used. At short range canister-shot had the same effect as machine-gun fire.

Men walking forward into this carnage displayed extraordinary courage. At Gettysburg, in July 1863, the Confederate 26th N. Carolina Regiment lost 708 out of 800 men. In the same battle, during the famous Pickett's Charge against Union lines, the Confederate's Virginia Brigade attacked 1,427 strong: just 486 men returned.

16

▽ Attacking regiments often sent two companies forward as "skirmishers" – scouts and snipers. Six companies followed in tight ranks; two waited behind in reserve.

▷ Rifle-musket bullets "dropped" a lot, so the rifleman aimed high. While attackers both close up and far away might be hit, there was always a "safe zone" in between.

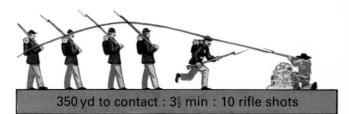

350 yd to contact : 3½ min : 10 rifle shots

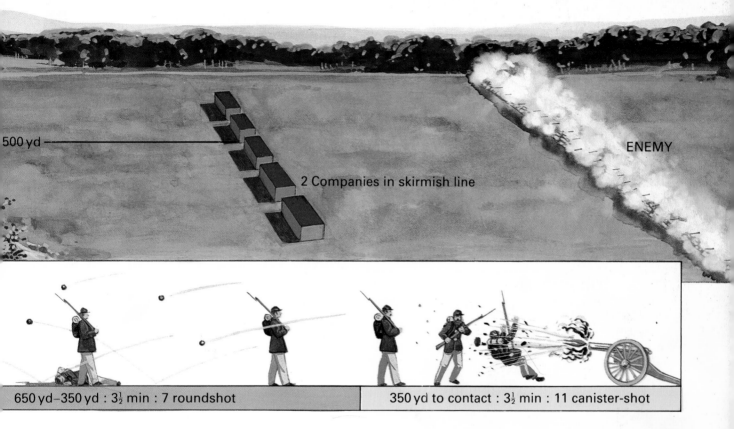

500 yd

ENEMY

2 Companies in skirmish line

650 yd–350 yd : 3½ min : 7 roundshot

350 yd to contact : 3½ min : 11 canister-shot

Because the old smooth-bore musket had been too inaccurate to hit anything but the biggest target, soldiers had been drawn up in tightly packed ranks. If they all fired together in the enemy's general direction, some of them were bound to hit something, more or less by accident. The Civil War rifle-musket was much more accurate and quicker to use; the shoulder-to-shoulder ranks now made easy targets, and so casualties were often dreadfully high.

Troops defending a position could take cover behind convenient banks or fences. Sometimes they had time to scrape shallow holes with their bayonets and to pile up low barricades of timber and stones for shelter. But the attackers were often marched slowly across wide open ground, suffering terrible casualties all the way. Because they were all supposed to arrive at the enemy's line at the same moment, they were not allowed to break their neat ranks and measured pace. They were only allowed to surge ahead in a charge at the very last minute – and by that time there might be few men left on their feet.

Holding the line

Defenders in a battle always enjoy advantages over attackers, because they can shelter from enemy fire behind cover. But the Civil War rifleman was by no means safe, or sure to win, even when he was defending a strong position. At the important Union victory of Gettysburg in July 1863 the Union troops fought almost entirely on the defensive. Yet although the Confederate army had casualties of one in every three, killed or wounded, the Northern army still lost one in five – a hideous cost for their victory. For example the Union's 24th Michigan Regiment alone lost 80 out of every 100 men. At the earlier battle of Antietam in September 1862 the defending 1st Texas Regiment of the Confederacy lost 82 out of every 100.

The reason was not just the courage of the attackers. Few men carried more than 40 cartridges, which ran out quite quickly, leaving them to defend themselves with bayonets and musket butts. Campaigns were often fought in wild country with only a few dirt roads. It was difficult for supply wagons to reach every part of an army strung out over large areas of woods and fields. On the battlefield itself, messages traveled no faster than a horseman. Often, generals did not realize that parts of their armies were in difficulty until it was too late to send more men or ammunition to the places where they were needed.

▽ Hard-pressed Union riflemen hold a low stone fence against Confederate charges. Many campaigns were fought over farming country like this, so marching was not too difficult. But some took place in wild forest or swampland, adding to the soldiers' hardships.

Each Union regiment had two flags: the national flag and a blue regimental flag.

Skirmishers and horse-holders

▽ Union cavalrymen dismount to form a skirmish line behind a rail fence. The horse-holders are leading their mounts to the rear. The troopers' short jackets are trimmed with the traditional yellow braid of American cavalry uniforms. One holds the guidon – the swallow-tailed squadron flag. This lucky unit is one of those issued with the seven-shot Spencer repeating carbine, so they can quickly lay down a storm of bullets. One man loads a tube of cartridges from a leather case into his carbine butt.

Union cavalry were not very effective in the first two years of the war. There were several reasons: one of them was simply that Northerners, in general, were not nearly such good riders as Confederates!

In the South, people rode every day. Many Northerners were more used to harnessing a horse to a plow than riding it across country for days on end. Before Union troopers learned how to maneuver in battle, they had to be taught how to ride – and, just as important, how to take care of their mounts, because horses are very prone to illness if not properly cared for. (A horse can even die if given too much water at the wrong time.)

As time passed, however, the Union put a large corps of fine cavalry into the field. Men like Generals Buford and Sheridan trained them to make the best use of their weapons and equipment, which were generally better than those of the poorer Southern army.

Union horsemen became very versatile – able to fight in different ways depending upon the conditions they found. They sometimes made old-fashioned charges, sabers in hand; but they were more often used as mounted infantry. This meant that they rode quickly to the spot where troops were needed, then dismounted and fought like infantry with their modern carbines. While three men out of every four formed this skirmish line, the fourth led their horses to the rear, where he waited under cover until the horses were needed again.

21

Artillery

The artillery which accompanied the Civil War horsemen and foot soldiers on campaign was important to the outcome of many battles. In the mid-nineteenth century new inventions and discoveries were starting to improve machines of all kinds. Cannons were no exception; and the first examples of newer and deadlier types of gun served alongside old, well-proven weapons. The results were often murderous for Civil War infantry who had to face enemy cannons.

The first rifled cannons were now coming into use. The principle was exactly the same as for the rifled musket: a spiral groove down the inside of the barrel spun the ball as it was fired, making it fly in a straight line.

The Union's industrial might gave it an advantage when it came to making these new guns; but in fact both sides used a mixture of cannons of many sizes and types, both rifled and smooth-bore. The most common of all was an old bronze-barreled smooth-bore called a Napoleon 12-pounder – a gun firing a shot weighing 12 lb (5.5 kg).

Most guns on both sides could fire a variety of different types of ammunition.

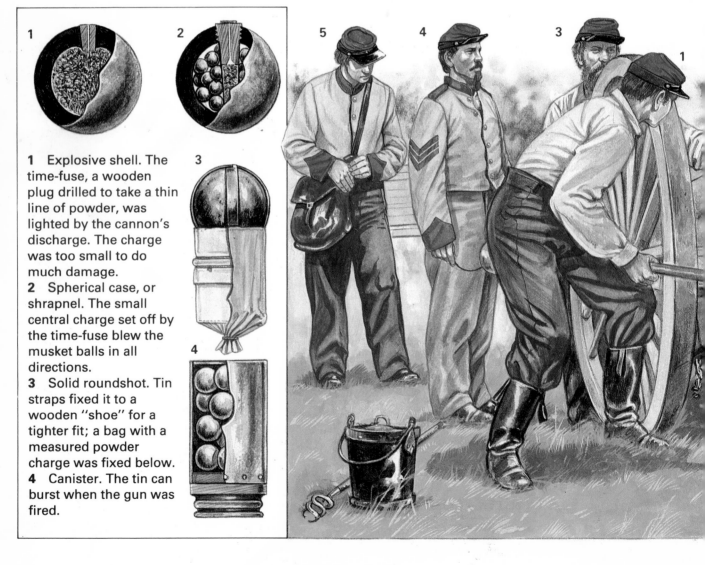

1 Explosive shell. The time-fuse, a wooden plug drilled to take a thin line of powder, was lighted by the cannon's discharge. The charge was too small to do much damage.

2 Spherical case, or shrapnel. The small central charge set off by the time-fuse blew the musket balls in all directions.

3 Solid roundshot. Tin straps fixed it to a wooden "shoe" for a tighter fit; a bag with a measured powder charge was fixed below.

4 Canister. The tin can burst when the gun was fired.

◁ A six-horse team with gun, limber and crew. Gun teams were hard to control and dangerous to other soldiers on the crowded country roads.

▽ Confederate Napoleon gun at the ready; the officer is in charge of this and one other gun. Crewman No.**1** has sponged out sparks from the last shot; No.**2** has put a shot in the muzzle, and No.**1** has rammed it home. No.**3** has pricked the powder bag through the touch hole and now covers the hole to stop accidental firing. No.**4** waits to fire, by pulling a cord from a striker device on the touch-hole. No.**5** brings the next shot.

Solid cannonballs, or roundshot, were fired at buildings, fortifications or tight-packed masses of infantry. Cannons called howitzers could lob explosive shells high in the air that exploded on the target when set off by a burning time-fuse. A variation was the shrapnel shell, set off in mid-air by a time-fuse, showering enemy infantry below with deadly musket balls. Most artillery fire was effective at ranges between 1,000 and 2,000 paces. At short range infantry and cavalry could be massacred by canister, a shower of big iron balls like a giant shotgun blast.

For traveling, cannon were hooked to two-wheeled ammunition carts, or limbers. A battery, or unit of six guns, with their limbers, ammunition, supply wagons and other gear needed nearly 100 horses. Moving artillery tore up the dirt roads dreadfully, adding summer dust and winter mud to the miseries of the marching infantry.

In battle, horses and wagons waited close behind the cannons. Enemy snipers and cannons often concentrated on gun crews and horse teams, with horrible results. At the battle of Spotsylvania a two-gun section of the Union 5th Artillery was silenced in moments. All the horses fell, as did 23 out of 24 men; the gun-carriages were completely splintered. The hail of bullets can be imagined by the 39 holes in a single bucket found lying beside the guns.

Repeating guns and electric signals

Many new scientific inventions played a part in the war. Apart from the use of trains to carry men and supplies quickly over long distances, the most important new advances were repeating rifles and electric telegraph signaling.

Union gunsmiths perfected the metal rifle cartridge. This held powder, bullet and percussion cap in one copper tube. It was weatherproof, easy to handle and safe to store.

▽ The Whitworth marksman's rifle had telescopic sights. Loaded with carefully handmade ammunition, it could put 20 shots into a 12-in (30-cm) circle at 500 yd (500 m). This is as accurate as a modern military rifle. This Union sniper calculates his range: the measured cord keeps the readings of the scale constant.

▷ Hydrogen balloons were used by observers to spy on enemy positions and to direct artillery fire. They signaled directions with semaphore flags or telegraph equipment. The balloon expert Professor Thaddeus Lowe made hundreds of ascents for the Union army. The hydrogen was made on the spot.

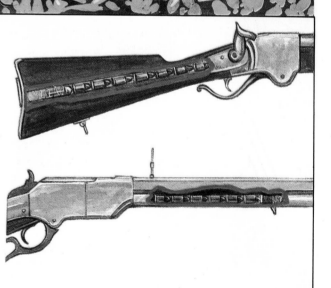

▷ The Spencer repeater (top) took a tube of 8 copper cartridges, loaded through the butt. In tests it fired 21 shots a minute, including changing tubes twice. The Henry rifle (bottom) could fire 15 cartridges from a magazine under the barrel in just 11 seconds. Both guns fed the next cartridge up into the breech when the trigger-guard lever was lowered and raised.

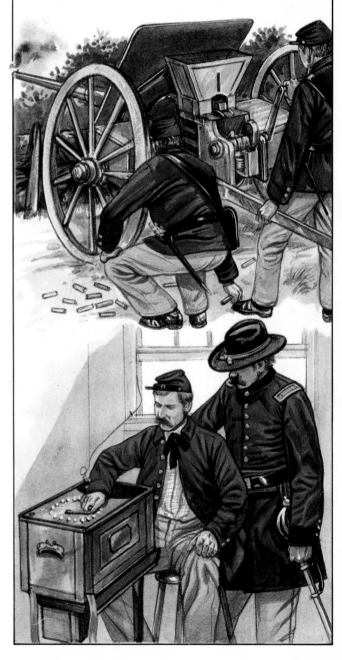

▽ The Civil War saw the first use of crude machine guns. They were not very effective: commanders had not yet worked out how to use them to advantage. One of the best was the Union Agar gun, nick-named "the coffee mill" from the brass funnel into which steel tubes loaded with powder, ball and percussion caps were fed. At Middlesburg, Virginia in March 1862 the 28th Pennsylvania Volunteers used two Agars to devastate attacks by Confederate cavalry.

It also led to the invention of repeating rifles: the metal cartridge could be passed through a feeding mechanism inside the gun that would have torn up paper cartridges. Confederates who met armed Union troops were greatly impressed with a gun which was apparently loaded in the morning and then fired all day.

Both sides used telegraph (**right**), which passed electric signals along wires. Union operators were civilian employees of the telegraph company – even generals were forbidden to see their code books!

Trench warfare

Most campaigns involved armies marching around the countryside, but there were a number of sieges and some areas of permanent fortifications. For nine long months in 1864–5, both sides fought in complex systems of trenches, dug-outs and batteries around the Confederate stronghold of Petersburg, Virginia. Eventually these were even longer than the Union defenses around Washington, which stretched 37 miles (60 km) with 68 forts and many smaller blockhouses.

These trenches were very similar to the ones used fifty years later in World War I. The walls, and sometimes the floors, were lined with timber. Both armies used mortars to lob shells into the enemy trenches, so "bomb-proof" shelters were roofed with heavy logs and earth. Trenches were even protected by wire entanglements to trip and delay attackers (although the wire was smooth – barbed wire was not invented until 1874). Explosive mines were buried out in front of the trenches, to be blown up if the enemy infantry attacked. If there was no time for anything more elaborate, a very effective barrier could be made simply by cutting down trees and laying them out in front of the defenses, with the tangled branches toward the enemy.

▷ Bird's-eye view of a trench system: (A) first line of trenches dug.
(B) "Saps," dug forward from first trench. When second trench (C) joins ends of saps, these are used as communication trenches for backward and forward movement under cover.
(D) Outposts, to fire on flanks of enemy attacks on main trenches.
(E) New sap being dug forward: eventually a third main trench will be dug in front of (C).
(F) Gun batteries.

Among the Union troops who fought with particular bravery at Petersburg were regiments of blacks. After declaring all slaves free in 1862, the North recruited some 186,000 blacks into the US Colored Troops.

▽ Men of the US Colored Infantry man winter trenches at Petersburg. They wear gum blankets or the Union army's sky blue caped greatcoat. The old sergeant carries "Ketcham's Grenades" – giant darts which exploded when the nose-plunger hit the ground. The 10-in (25-cm) mortar could throw a 5-lb (2-kg) shell up to 2,000 yd (1,800 m).

Medical services

At the outbreak of war the US Army Medical Department numbered just 115 men; of these 27 went south to join the Confederates. Surgeons did their best for the wounded and sick during the Civil War, but they were always terribly overworked. Most medical officers were civilian doctors who joined their state volunteer regiments. Much of the care for the wounded who survived long enough to reach a hospital was given by voluntary civilian organizations like today's Red Cross.

The causes of infection were still not properly understood. There were even doctors who believed that gangrene – a deadly infection of dirty or badly healed wounds – was caused by damp evening air. The instruments used for operations and the bandages put on wounds were used over and over again without proper cleaning.

Overworked surgeons, faced with the horrible wounds caused by the big, rather slow bullets of those days, often cut off arms and legs which would have healed with modern treatment. Although there were now drugs to dull the agony of operations, many men died of shock or infection after surgery.

In fact, far more men died from disease than wounds. In the Union army 204,100 men died as a result of wounds, but 284,000 from disease. The worst killers were typhoid, dysentery and pneumonia – just what one would expect among unwashed soldiers crammed together, with bad food, bad water, and no proper shelter from the cold and damp. The Civil War rifleman's deadliest enemy was not a bullet or shell but an invisible germ.

▷ Union divisional hospital. Wounded were given hasty first aid by their regiment's doctor. They then made their way back to the division's hospital, often dragging themselves there on foot. There were few horse-drawn ambulances, and the civilian drivers were often lazy and cowardly. If the wounded survived serious surgery, they were then moved – on trains or, as here, on river steamers – to hospitals far behind the lines for long-term treatment.

Many doctors were dedicated, though still ignorant of the need to keep the instruments and bandages clean to prevent infection. But medical orderlies – the unskilled helpers – were often callous, thieving rogues.

Medical staff often wore green braid or badges on their uniforms, like this New York stretcher-bearer.

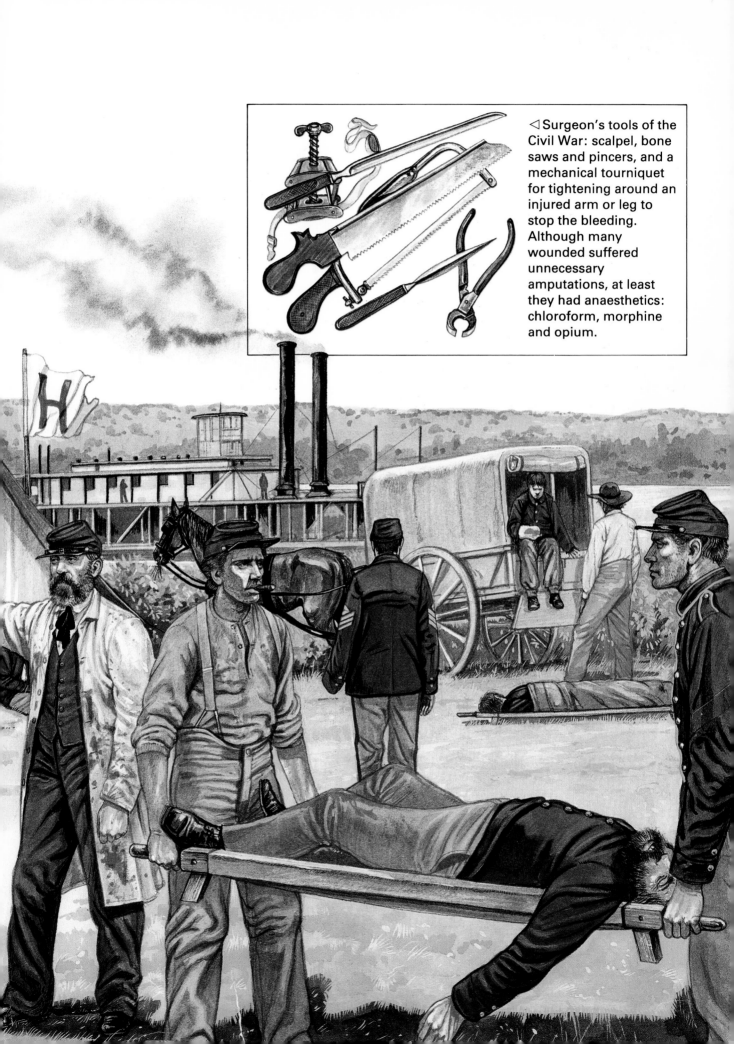

◁ Surgeon's tools of the Civil War: scalpel, bone saws and pincers, and a mechanical tourniquet for tightening around an injured arm or leg to stop the bleeding. Although many wounded suffered unnecessary amputations, at least they had anaesthetics: chloroform, morphine and opium.

Glossary

Battery *Either* a unit of about six cannons; *or* the fortified position on which they are placed.

Brigade Group of regiments under a single commander.

Canister shot Tin can of iron balls fired from a cannon; the can burst open when the cannon was fired.

Carbine Short rifle or musket used by horsemen.

Cartridge Tube of paper or metal holding the powder and bullet for a single loading of a gun.

Company Unit of about 100 soldiers; several companies made up a regiment.

Corporal Junior army rank, usually one grade senior to the common privates; marked by two stripes on the sleeve.

Corps Large military formation of several divisions under a single commander.

Division Large military formation of several brigades under a single commander.

Fatigue uniform Simple clothing worn for daily chores – and often in battle.

General Very senior officer. Major-generals often commanded divisions or corps; lieutenant-generals, corps or armies; generals, whole armies.

Grenade Small hand-thrown bomb.

Howitzer Short-barreled cannon used for lobbing shells through the air at a high angle to fall steeply on the target.

Limber Two-wheeled ammunition cart to which a cannon was hitched.

Lock (gun) The firing mechanism.

Militia Part-time soldiers; civilians who report for training at intervals.

Mortar Very short-barreled cannon, often small, used for lobbing shells steeply over short ranges.

Muzzle The open end of a gun barrel.

Percussion cap Explosive pellet in copper casing shaped like a tiny top hat, used to set off the main charge in a gun.

Regiment Military unit, made up of a number of companies, under a single commander.

Rifled gun Musket or cannon with spiral grooving down the inside of the barrel, to spin the bullet or ball in flight, thus keeping it in a straight line.

"Sack" jacket Simple working jacket issued to Union troops, so called from its shapeless cut!

"Sap" Zig-zag length of trench dug forward toward enemy lines.

Sergeant Junior military rank, in charge of a few corporals and two or three dozen soldiers; marked by three sleeve stripes.

Sharps rifle Breech-loading, accurate rifle invented by Sharps and used by some special units of the Union army.

Shell Exploding missile fired from cannon.

Shrapnel Type of shell which burst in mid-air, showering troops below with balls or shards; named after its inventor.

Smooth-bore A gun without a rifled barrel; less accurate than a rifle.

Sniper A marksman who picks off the enemy at long range.

Touch hole The hole in the breech of a muzzle-loading gun, connecting the main powder charge in the barrel with the small priming explosive which sets it off.

Timechart

April 12, 1861 War begins when Southerners shell Union-held Fort Sumter, South Carolina.

July 21, 1861 Union advance on Confederate capital of Richmond, Virginia, driven back at Bull Run ("First Manassas").

March–June 1862 Outnumbered Confederate General Stonewall Jackson wins brilliant Shenandoah Valley campaign by rapid marches and cunning deception.

April 6, 1862 Indecisive Battle of Shiloh costs a total of 24,000 casualties.

April–May 1862 Union General McClellan's advance on Richmond bogs down in Peninsula Campaign.

June 1862 Confederate General Robert E. Lee pushes Union army north again in Seven Days' Campaign.

August 30, 1862 Lee and Jackson beat Union General Pope at Battle of "Second Manassas."

September 17, 1862 Invading the North, Lee is attacked at Antietam, which costs worst losses of any single day of the war: about 12,400 Union, 13,700 Confederate.

December 13, 1862 Advancing southward, Union General Burnside is defeated at Fredericksburg.

May 1, 1863 Lee's 43,000 Confederates beat Union General "Fighting Joe" Hooker's 70,000 Union troops at Chancellorsville – but Stonewall Jackson is accidentally shot by one of his own sentries.

July 1–3, 1863 Advancing northward again, Lee fights Union General Meade at Gettysburg. In three dreadful days, ending with the costly failure of General Pickett's attack on Union lines, the Rebels suffer losses from which they never really recover: 31,000 casualties.

July 4, 1863 After a long siege, Union General Grant takes Vicksburg, the Confederate stronghold on the Mississippi.

September 1863 Confederate victory at Battle of Chickamauga.

November 1863 Union Generals Grant and Sherman defeat Confederates at Chattanooga.

March 1964 Ulysses S. Grant is named supreme Union commander.

May 1864 Grant invades the South. Lee fights brilliantly in "the Wilderness," at Spotsylvania and at Cold Harbor. But unlike previous Union generals, Grant simply changes direction and keeps advancing. The Union army is now much larger and better equipped than the dwindling Confederate forces, and time is on Grant's side.

May 11, 1864 Confederate cavalry leader General Jeb Stuart is mortally wounded at Yellow Tavern.

June 18, 1864 Lee's Army of Northern Virginia is pinned down in trench lines defending Petersburg and Richmond.

September 1, 1864 Union General Sherman forces Confederate retreat from Atlanta, Georgia.

November–December 1864 Sherman marches from Atlanta to Savannah, destroying Southern crops and stores throughout Georgia.

April 1, 1865 Grant's victory at Five Forks forces Lee to abandon Petersburg and Richmond the next day.

April 9, 1865 Lee is forced to surrender his last 7,800 men at Appomattox, Virginia. The war ends.

April 17, 1865 President Lincoln is assassinated.

Index

PRINTED IN BELGIUM BY
proost
INTERNATIONAL BOOK PRODUCTION